BEAUTY FROM THE PAIN

EMOTIONS

ASTHA KHARYA

Made with ♥ on the Notion Press Platform
www.notionpress.com

All thanks to the situations of my life.

Situations help me to find a poet inside me.

KYU HAI ITNI PARESHANIA

KYU HEIN ITNE GHUM

KYA ISLIYE DUNIYA MEIN AAYE HUM HEIN

ESA BHALA KONSA KAIDA TOOTA HAI

HUMSE ZINDAGI KA

JO HAR SHUKH RUTHA HAI

HUMSE ZINDAGI KA

KHAUF SI LAGTI HAI ZINDAGI

DAR SATATA HAR DUM HAI

KYA ISLIYE DUNIYA MEIN AAYE HUM HEIN

UMEED TO KOI REHTI NAHI

DO PAL BHI KHUSHIYAN SANG REHTI NAHI

MUSKILON KE DHAAGE ULAZTE HEIN JADA

AB KHULTE TO KAM HEIN

KYA ISLIYE DUNIYA MEIN AAYE HUM HEIN........

- ME

.......Otherwise , I wouldn't have come across the poet in me

Contents

Contents

Preface

I write poems about what is actually going on in my life. I write just to feel relax from my unknowingly thoughts. I started to write poems in 2018. I have met many people in my life who have left me at the end and from them I have learnt many lessons. I am that type of person who trusts very easily, gets attached easily, can do anything just to make others happy without even thinking about myself and always got hurt at the end. Whenever I share my feelings, my emotions, real me with anyone they always end up hurting me. Everyone treats me like an option in their life I am not anyone's priority nor as important as I thought. So I decided to stop sharing my emotions to anyone and start writing just for the sake of my peace.

I had my reasons to pick this option.

I write......

I write,becausc I know there is no restriction to write my feelings out.

I write,because my pen is the sole weapon that I put trust on.

The ink is the fuel of my feelings, and I can make it a perfect drawing with words, no matter what the content is.

Every profession is precious , but the writer's is much more precious than that, even diamond has no chance of beating someone's inked feelings.

I realized I would be gone some day, and I wanted to leave behind something that would continue to tell my story.....I wanted to share my poems to everyone in my own way.

1. Live it like you mean

Don't be sure, You'll find cure,
You are the naive, Make a strive
So what there is no joy, Be your own decoy,
Have a glance, Don't look for a chance!!!
Live it like you mean, Enjoy it like you mean
Don't wish , take a step, Make all the prep,
Drudgery will always exist,
It's a challenge for you to persist,
Some things won't matter a lot,
But they are needed to make you float,
Life is the dance, Don't look for a chance,
Live it like you mean, Enjoy it like you mean
You experience pain, it keeps you sane,
Your body is heaven, Love it as it is brethren,
You are alive, Then why fear to take a dive,
You smile, You cry,
But always make a try
This you need to enhance,
'Because you may never get another chance '
So, ***live it like you mean, enjoy it like you mean***
Live it like you mean, Enjoy it like you mean....

2. Destiny

Does destiny always stay,
If not, then are we right to blame our destiny
We all are confused between destiny and our success.
We all are confused between winning and blaming destiny for not winning.
We all are confused between falling in love with destiny name and getting broken with destiny name.
Stop it guys, destiny is something which is already written or which can be written by ourselves.
But we are so super talented that without thinking in seconds we blame dating for everything that has
happened or are going to happen.
It's our choice whether to keep destiny with ourself or to write destiny with our own hands.
Because whatever that has happened or going to happen wrong is by our mistake or we have not tried at
all.
At last all I want to tell is that destiny is beautiful because whatever is going to happen is what we are
doing right now....

3. Live Every Moment

For the few moments of life,
Is it fair to get lost in that moment.
Life has its own rules,
Some call their life as short,
And some call it as big
But we all get few moments in life.
Where we have to either create it or,
Either make it a memory.
After all , for the few moments of life.
We all have to just get lost in that moment,
Because the moment can be anything with anyone
Whether its with so called friend,
Or whether its with bestfriend,
Maybe it can be with soulmate,
Or with an online person,
Because moments are beautiful,
And people are unique.
Love life, because
" Do pal ki zindagi hai yaar, Jeelo aur kya "

4. Decide Yourself

Who says, life can't be excited ??
Better decide yourself , you want to play or exit.
Better decide yourself , you want to enjoy or waste your time.
Better decide yourself, you want problems or solutions to every problem.
Better decide yourself, you want your or others thought.
When you get answers to this, then I am sure you will be thinking about life forever.

5. Dreams

Dreams destroying my sleep
How can hurt reach so much ?
Waking up is too much effort
Sleep is luxury I can't afford
Depression overwhelms my soul
Deep darkness , a big , black hole
Sadness eats it way through my heart
Where does it end ? Where does it start ?
Noone can understand this pain
Nothing to lose, Nothing to gain
Lost in a never ending maze
Every moment just a dizzy daze
Why does it have to me ?
If only the future I could see
Afraid of shadows in the dark
Will I ever make my mark ?
Unseen tears flowing from my heart
I must go on, play my part
Life has to continue for today
Living my life, come what may....
So much to be thankful for
How can I ask for many more?

I just wish this could go away
For me to have a natural day...
So tired of fighting this feeling
My mind just reeling
I hate these pills I have to take
Makes me feel my life is just a fake
What can I do ? Where can I go ?
Stumbling around to and fro
Wondering when this will end
Not much more to say for now
Just wondering when this will end
Not much more to say for now
Just wondering how, how , how
Again pulling myself together
Hoping this will last forever.........

6. Everything Ends

A dried leaf , detached from its genesis
And so detached are all its dreams
Some precious green fantasies it saw
Were devastated by the autumn bow
To the spring god, its question of pain
" Why do you show me dreams , if all has to go in vain ? "
The lord smiled and said, accepting its bends
" Nothing lasts forever, Everything ends. "

7. Happiness

When the sun rises in the morning scatters the smile of light,
Meets everyone's soul and drive away the darkness filling bright
Happiness is color which showers like rain.
Happiness is a goal that see in a face again & again.
Happiness is a song singing everytime.
Happiness is a book takes me to the divine.
Happiness lies in music , one we dance & sing with friends.
Happiness lies in everything , it shines everyone's heart.
Happiness lies in self image , that is drawn by art.
The garden blossoms with laughter of flowers,
Whose smell spread everywhere,
Comes through lots of fame and embrace,
Which doesn't allow you to go anywhere.

8. Lie

To everything that was said to be done,
All was said & nothing was ever done.
Sinking in my life....
Somewhere beneath the sea
I drowned alone in my loneliness
Probably no one could see.
Busy in their lives, happening
Or maybe not so happening
They still have more people than
My whole life has been enduring
Who am I to complain
I am sick and about to crumble
But they tell me that's what life is
Alone you have to step up
And alone you have to stumble
How hilarious the word echo
"I will be there for you always"
When they don't even know
If tomorrow I am gonna exist, Anyways....

9. A Lonely Star

A lonely star sits in the sky.
It begins to flicker and begins to cry.
A lonely star looks down on us all.
It takes a step and starts to fall.
A lonely star falling down like a apple from a tree.
It still wears a frown.
A lonely star laying on the ground.
It looks to the moon,
A home it never found.
A lonely star blinks her goodbye's.
Her light goes out and she slowly dies....

10. A Girl

There is a girl who sits in the corner.
Her heart is crying out.
There are people all around her.
But noone seems to hear her shout.
Her life was once happy.
Full of friends and care.
She was always laughing.
There was always someone there.
But now her life seems empty.
What's missing, she doesn't know.
She wears a mask everyday.
Her true feelings she doesn't show.
Her once colorful and cheerful life.
Has turned so dull and grey.
She once enjoyed her group of friends.
Now she just wishes them away.
For when she is by herself,
She can break free from her shell.
She can let the unhappiness break free.
And unleash the devil from hell.
Because at the end of the day,
When everyone's in their beds asleep,

The misery surrounds her,
And the pain , it cuts so deep.
She wants someone to listen.
Someone to understand.
But when she opens up.
Nobody wants to lend a hand.
So she waits until the sun finally sets.
To open up once more.
This time it's no longer in words,
But it results in terrible sores.
These sores cry their tears at night.
The tears aren't transparent but a deathly red.
As they cry, she feels a release.
From the terrible pain in her head.
Some people would say she is crazy.
Some people would say she is mad.
But she can't resist the temptation when it arrives.
Even though she knows its bad.
Noone will ever understand this urge.
It's something she can't explain.
She feels shame for the scars on her body.
But always ends up doing it again.
You see , this girl is a victim,
Of something she can't comprehend.
Deep in her heart she knows she must stop.
For her life she doesn't want to end.
But for now it's the only way she knows.

To stop feeling the loss of friendship and care.
Because at the moment she is invisible.
Noone notices she's there..........

11. Emptiness

I want it all to stop.
I don't wanna feel this emptiness.
This emotional void.
No, I don't wanna be numb.
My depression is like the uninvited guest.
It's the monster below my bed.
It's always with me like the shadow in days.
Until it's all dark again.
My anxiety is a shape shifter,
Sometimes it's as small as a water droplet,
And other times it's the deepest ocean.
I want it all to stop.
I don't wanna live with no colors.
Nothing makes sense anymore.
Not even what I am writing I guess,
It's just me, penning down the hollowness.
The hollowness even I don't know.
It's like the black hole.
Until its gone.
I don't want to feel this.
I don't want to be just another sad soul living with the truest smile.

I want it to stop....

12. Why Am I So Wrong?

Why am I so wrong ?
No matter whatsoever the situation,
No matter whatsoever the relation,
Either it's family or friends,
Either it's neighbor or relatives.
But its me who is always wrong,
No matter whatsoever the age gap,
Either big or small.
But its me who is always wrong,
I do confess mistakes even when I ain't wrong,
When its someone elder than me,
Just as a token of respect that you thought me,
I do confess mistakes even when I ain't wrong,
When its someone younger than me,
Just as a token of kind and care,
Because you taught me to humble,
But why I'm always wrong ?
I too need respect,
I too need kindness and care,
I am just tired of being wrong,

Ain't I stressed ?
Ain't I tensed ?
Ain't I frustrated ?
Maybe I don't pretend like one,
Because I always learned from you,
To never fade that smile,
I know I'm messed up,
But I'm not always wrong,
Sometimes I feel like going away,
Far from this world,
Sometimes I feel like ending up,
But escaping from situations isn't my cup of tea,
It isn't what my dad taught me,
I am his lioness,
Brave and valiant,
Strong enough to combat all those blames,
But I get exhausted,
Because I cannot always be wrong....
Because I cannot always be wrong.....

13. As If

What does it feel like
As if sayings drilled
Within your bones
As if you can't withstand yourself
Whatever you do is wrong
And sadness is the only emotion you got
You feel out of control
As if you are trapped
Lake in the big ocean
Chilled bones are part of conversations
As if your every part of body cries
As if you can't fight
As if it has been made your part
As if.........
As ifs are not going to end...............

14. We All Tried

We are all alone
We have the heart of stone
We are here to make our name
We all cried because of the pain
We live our life with faith
We are still alive
That's great
Many of us tried to himself or herself
Looks like they forgot
God is always on our side
We have beaten our saitaan
All the happiness we felt
Because of the small steps
We have taken
We are all left alone
By the people we loved
Maybe they are the reason
We are so fucked up
Many of us cried
Some of us died
But at the end of the day
We all tried.........

15. Something In My Mind

Living in conflict
Aggravation in heart
Moisture in eyes
Stuck in defoliation
Darkness overshadowed
Haunted by pain
Brain is exploding
Being demolished
Soul lost the peace
Pain breaks boundaries
Someone's words are stuck in the heart like thorns
Now I want to run away from this chaos to a place where I can enjoy the silence......

16. Let's Just For Once

Let's not think much, my soul
Let's just forget and move on in life
Let's just smile rather than being sad
Let's just complete those story which we left incomplete
Let's not think much about life
Let's just try to enjoy it
Let's just make our loved one's happy
Specially our soul which is much more depressed,
Let's at least try to make our soul happy
Once again, let's make our life happy in this tough situation
Let's just cry over those talks or things which hurt
Let's just forget and forgive the one's
Let's just take a new step with every breathe
Let's just love, smile and make life wonderful.....

17. I

I really don't know why,
Sometimes I want to cry a loud,
I wish to scream and shout,
And let all my feelings out.
Inside my bones I'm trapped,
And with a skin cover I'm wrapped,
Within myself I do hide,
I feel no pain or joy inside.
My life has come to a pause,
In silence my days all pass,
My heart has turned to numb,
I'm just waiting for the end to come.
With no more hopes and trust to persist,
My dreams have ceased to exist,
With no more paths to follow,
My heavy heart is now a hollow.
With loneliness all alone,
I can feel my tears rolling down,
I really don't know why,
Sometimes silence makes me cry a loud...........

18. Silence

Heart shouts the pain aloud,
But nobody is here around.
Even though in the background playing is the song,
Not a single beat syncing along.
Who will try to find the meaning behind this,
It's warm place still
I feel sick.
Unseen yet forecasted pain is worrying me,
Silently under the silence,
Not a single voice set free.........

19. Emotions To Hold On

They tell me about how they are disturbed,
I keep listening to them sitting in the corner of my room.
Trying my best to hold my emotions,
To tame that tsunami.
Cluster of emotions in my head,
And everything around me somehow like the scenes of the worst storms.
Black clouds surrounded, strong winds,
And there I'm, in the middle of the ocean,
Trying to sail my boat through it.
Sometimes I just feel like it's all in my head,
May be all I need is an escape.
Something real to cling onto,
Or the sun to shine.
I sit there still,
Just trying to figure out that escape.
Just to feel okay,
To not be in my head.
I zone in to their voice again telling me about their problems,
And I listen to them sitting numb in my corner.

20. Have Faith In Yourself

Believe in yourself,
Destiny has everything planned.
Stop believing in visualized things,
Those are just the distractions
Moving towards negativity.
Eat what you love eating,
Drink what you love drinking,
Travel the places you love travelling,
Nothing is impossible if you work hard for it.
Tomorrow is a way too far,
Live today , Secure tomorrow.
Stop believing in superstition,
You'll get what is planned by the God,
You can't get beyond that.
Trust yourself, trust almighty.
Stop believing what makes you sad,
Enjoy this life, it's all yours.
Beware of people, trust the correct ones,
Ask your sixth sense before trusting someone,
That's all you need to do to smile.

21. A Girl With Broken Heart

A smile on face,
A shine in eyes,
An anger on nose,
But she was a broken heart.
Might be everyone is thinking,
She is suffering from breakup.
But please hold on everyone,
She is suffering from broken friendship.
She is broken from heart.
But strong enough from mind.
A broken friendship,
Explained all the things which she suffered.
Though she learnt everything now,
About friendship which was just fake.
Those feelings, enjoyment, attachments everything etc....
And left with a tag , ***"A Girl With Broken Heart"*** *.*

22. You Are Not A Loser

You are not loser my dear,
You are actually bigger than the rest,
You are braver than the rest calling you a loser , for there is a shallowness in them which are yet to find in them,
They have not seen the real you,
They have not seen that YOU which you have kept only to yourself
They have not seen how brave you are with all emotions lying inside of you and yet how you face them every morning with a smile on your face,
My dear you are not a loser they call you so far they have not seen you behaving more maturely than the human actually listening,
You are ignoring them & not replying with harsh words because you care about them.
YOU ARE NOT A LOSER MY DEAR.......

23. Does Bestfriend Also Change

Those long phone calls,
Are getting to short everyday.
Is this the end of forever ?
Does bestfriend also make their way ?
The endless drama, the gossips,
And those tears of laughter in the eye.
Where should I find all this ?
Does bestfriend also lie ?
The motivational lectures after a heart break,
Hating the same person together.
What is the one thing I miss ?
Does bestfriend also find another friend ?
The small fights on a daily basis,
Every secret gets a pinky promise,
Where should I speak my heart out ?
Does best friend also dismiss ?
The blackmail of ***' Dost dost na raha '*** *is no more,*
Ignorance is now a threat.
To whom should I dedicate ***' Tera yaar hu main '*** *?*
Does bestfriend also forget ?

The shoulder to cry on is missing,
My personal clown is no where,
Is this the bitter truth ?
Does bestfriend also not care ?
The one who knows me better than myself,
Now is acting so strange.
Is this reality of life ?
Does bestfriend also change ?

24. I Was At Fault

In this journey of life,
I was at fault when -
I assumed venomous people were mine,
I assumed fake ones as mine,
I thought I was at cloud nine,
But then I realized I was in a line.....
I was at fault when -
I presumed that you had time for me,
I presumed that you could sacrifice for me,
I thought that for every lock, you're the key,
But now you are not my cup of tea....
I was at fault when -
I believed you were my true friend,
I thought you'll never let me cry,
But now it is time to say you good bye.....
I thought for your good, even in my bad times,
I thought for your best, even at my worst,
I'm sorry for all the efforts, I put after your ignorance,
But still I was at fault.......

25. Sometimes I Wonder

Sometimes I wonder the path I have chosen is right or wrong.
Sometimes I wonder the things I am doing is right or wrong.
Sometimes I wonder will this path that I am walking in, lead me to my destination.
I don't know what is going on,
I don't know where I will end up.
But I am just determined to move on,
I will not stop because of people pulling me back,
I will not stop because I am hurt,
I will not stop because I sometimes lose,
I will stop that day when I will find my goals accomplished.......

26. Life Is All About

Life is not always perfect,
Sometimes you learn and sometimes you teach,
Sometimes you suffer and sometimes you overcome,
Everything in life does not happen for the sake of enjoyment,
Sometimes it's the matter of good and bad,
Life never change without changing yourself,
That's what life is all about......

27. Nobody Owns Me

Nobody owns me,
I own myself !!
Why should I listen someone's advice ?
If it hurts me or supress me what I feel,
Because I know,
I have the right to make decisions for my life !!
However it's my life ,
Let me face the trauma,
Let me have the perks,
Whatever decision I make,
I somehow it's going to effect,
The good, the bad
Whatever it will be,
Atleast I will not blame anyone !!
Whatever decision I will make ,
At the end,
I am the one who has to live !!!!!!

28. For Maa Papa

Where do you get the strength ?
To remind us every single day.
How strong we are !
How we can conquer the world !
If and only if we want, we may, someday.....
Where do you get the positivity ?
To encourage us every single time,
We have fallen down before the finish line or accepted defeat in between.
Expect our win which we can't even begin to dream......
Where do you get the patience ?
To listen to our jokes, lies and stories.
About someone you may or may not know,
About things you may or may not care.
How do you always manage to always listen not just hear ?............

29. Myself

It's been a while since I last sat with myself
Life seems to be moving ahead faster
The ups and downs don't bother me as much nowadays, and it's probably odd
From feeling so much to so little
I am not sure if this is the maturity I hoped for
I look at people with the prettiest faces and the most hollow souls
Individuals who are so apart yet somehow together
And then there are people with souls intertwined yet so distant
It's moment like these I avoid nowadays
When all the things emotions I compress come out louder
To all the things I try not to see
Stand in front of me so loud
My mind almost numb and my hands jotting down everything I don't even realize
It's been a while since I last sat with myself
Life seems to be a rat trap,
Everything is moving faster towards the same direction in the utmost silence
And somehow I stand towards the opposite direction, with everyone crossing me faster and faster

I see them each day becoming numb, losing parts of themselves
they embraced
Loving people they shouldn't in the process not to hate themselves
To feel atleast something
It's been a while with the chaos overpowering......

30. Everyone I Loved

I feel as if everyone I have ever loved will be gone,
Either by distance and misunderstandings or death,
I know change is inevitable,
But I also know that I wanted some people to be a part of my life always,
But I could see them leaving while they said ***"Everything is as it is was"*** *,*
Whilst I could feel the change in my bones,
I fight for people a 100 times and they show me 101th time why I should not have fought for them,
Yet I fight,
Why do I feel as if I bother everyone when I know that's not the truth.
The ever rising covid cases have given rise to all negativities,
Never had we ever thought that we would need contacts in cemeteries,
The news is horrifying,
We need to be less aware.
Why do I laugh when I tell something important?
May be I fear the reaction?
I do feel a burden sometimes,
No one's been there when they said they will be,

I used to fight for attention,
Now, I like being on my own.
Losing someone close does changes something deep inside you,
But you know you aren't the same person with all your pieces anymore,
You see them with new friends,
Not bothered about you,
Or atleast pretending to be,
And here while writing this,
I wonder how much time will it take for me to really get over,
Not get a single thought of you the whole wide day,
And let go of that blurred hope that one day you will come back tired from the world ......

Printed by Libri Plureos GmbH in Hamburg, Germany

9 798889 513339